D0840177

Thanks to :
Conseil Général du Var
Mairie de Saint-Maximin
            for financial aid
Bernadette Fornalczyk
            for english translation

ASSOCIATION DES AMIS DE LA BASILIQUE SAINTE-MARIE-MADELEINE
DE SAINT-MAXIMIN-LA-SAINTE-BAUME
25, AVENUE DU MARÉCHAL-FOCH 83470 SAINT-MAXIMIN

SARL ÉDISUD, LA CALADE, RN 7, 3 120 ROUTE D'AVIGNON
13090 AIX-EN-PROVENCE − FRANCE
Tél. 04 42 21 61 44/Fax 04 42 21 56 20
www. edisud. com − e. mail : commercial@edisud. com

ISBN 2-7449-0449-6

SAINT-MAXIMIN-LA SAINTE-BAUME

THE BASILICA
SAINT MARY-MAGDALENE
AND THE ROYAL CONVENT

Michel MONCAULT

English edition by
Association des amis de la Basilique.

Édisud

En Tóuteis aquélei que nous an preceda :

Umblis Incouneigu,

Mounge fervènt

Rèi bastissèire,

qu'an adu, Chascun à sa Mesuro

uno pèiro à n'aquéu meravihous

Edifice, dins uno memo veneracien

Pèr la

Mario-Madaleno Benesido :

Aquest oubrage es dedica. *

* Dédication in provençal sub-dialect, " le maritime ",
spoken in Saint-Maximin-La Sainte-Baume.

The edition of « the basilica saint-mary Magdalene and the royal convent », by Michel Moncault, in 1985, brought an important stone to the knowledge about this outstanding architectural lot.

Indeed, very few towns in Provence can pride themselves on such a beautiful gothic architecture.

We are pleased to back up the reedition of this guide by the « Association des Amis de la Basilique ».

We hope it will, still, keep you company, long after you stopped in this high place of meditation, of prayer and culture.

Horace Lanfranchi,
Président du Conseil général du Var

COUVENT DE SAINT MAXIMIN
Plan général

Echelle de 0.002 pour 1 mètre

Ancienne infirmerie

Sacristie

Salle Capitulaire

Salle Commune

Réfectoire

Réfectoire

Cuisine primitive

Préau.

Ancienne hôtellerie

Cour du Collège.

Ancien Collège

Ancien Cimetière.

Ancien Cimetière

Base du Clocher

Art. H. Olivier C. Deuilliers 14 Marseille.

Plan général du couvent et de la basilique.

INTRODUCTION
TO THE THIRD ÉDITION

The Basilica of Saint Maximin was once called the "Third Tomb of Christianity" after Jerusalem and Rome, by the renovator of the theological convent, Father Lacordaire, in his book "The Life of Mary Magdalene", published in 1859. So this is no ordinary monument. It is a giant shrine to what remains of Mary Magdalene, the "Apostle of Apostles" as she was called by the fathers of the Church.

The new edition of this excellent work was written by Solange Rostan, who left us in 1989. She was the descendant of a dynasty of scholars, historians of Saint Maximin, who authored many works which have influence even today.

And by Father Michel Moncault, former priest of Saint Maximin, general vicary of the Diocese of Frejus-Toulon, who gave us leave to publish this book, and left us in 2002, too.

The Basilica

The excavations carried out in 1993 and 1994 by Mr. Jean Guyon, Mr. Michel Fixot and Mr. François Carrazé allowed us to discover a primitive building which must have served as a church in ancient times (5th century) upon which was built a baptistery, perhaps in the 6th century A.D., accessible from the church by three doors. These discoveries were of course very important to our understanding of the origins of Saint Maximin.

There was, of course, on a neighbouring hill, a "castrum", or cluster of villages, leagued together and called "Redonas", along with many farms on the surrounding plain, developed in Gallo-Roman times and renamed "Villa Lata" by the Romans.

The discovery of this baptistery, a few dozen metres from the oratory constructed to shelter the remains of Mary Magdalene and some of her companions, proves there was a Christian life active from the time of Constantine (4th Cent.). It should be noted that the ground level of the current crypt of the basilica is at approximately the same as that of the baptistery. It is therefore reasonable to think that, owing to the natural rise of the grounds, the primitive oratory became the crypt, and that the basilica was constructed on top.

The Royal Convent

The convent was sold by the Dominicans in 1959 when they transferred the noviciate to Toulouse. It was first purchased by an association of benefactors who founded a "School of Contemporary Exchange" devoted to spiritual and cultural activity. Then the Department of the Var and the city of Saint Maximin took back most of it and founded a society of mixed economies, "Le Clos", which then rented the building to France-Patrimoine, who converted the royal convent into a hotel: L'Hôtellerie du Couvent Royal. However, the visit to the cloister, the chauffoir, the refectory, the atrium, and the chapel is free of charge. And now… look at the photographs, read attentively the text in this opuscule, and you will see that the basilica reveals many treasures.

Michel ROY

Founder of the Association "Friends of the Basilica"
Honorary President

THE BASILICA
OF SAINT MARY OF MAGDALA

ORIGIN

This grand monument was raised by the explicit will of Charles II d'Anjou, Count of Provence, to the honour and glory of the Beneficent Mary Magdalene. Its foundation goes back to the ancient and venerable tradition of Provence, according to which, Mary Magdalene, sinner of the Gospel, sister of Martha and Lazarus, victim of persecution, like other disciples of Christ, at the hands of the Jews against the first Christians, would have come with her companions to preach the new faith in Provence, following Jesus'command, "Go forth and preach the Gospel to all creatures… In the name of the Father, and of the Son, and of the Holy Spirit"1. After many long years of penitence in the wild cavern at Sainte Baume, Mary Magdalene, told by Heaven of her imminent death, started a long journey towards the place where Saint Maximin, first Bishop of Aix, had raised an oratory, "Rodanas" or "Rodani". The legend tells us: The angels transported her and left her not far from La Voie Aurelienne, at the place where, in the next centuries, a column called the "Saint Pilon" would be erected to preserve the memory of these events (in 1463).

After a last communion, taken from the hand of the Holy Pontiff, she, herself, was taken by the hand of God. She was buried at the exact place where the basilica stands today.

Prince Charles de Salerne, son of Charles I d'Anjou, king of Naples and Sicily, Count of Provence, brother of Saint Louis, did not ignore the traditions of Provence.

In 1279, he ordered the excavations to find the remains of the "Beneficent Magdalene", lost since

Bas-relief at the altar of the rosary

Coat of arms
of the royal house
of Provence-Anjou-
Sicily-Jerusalem.
Cornerstone
of the basilica.

Personal seal of Charles I
of Anjou-Sicily,
Count of Provence.

Cire rouge
double attache de soie jaune et rouge

3

S. KAROLI II, REG. SICIL. COM. PROVINCIE.
(S. D. N° 4)

the Saracens invasion in the 8th century. Effectively, to protect these precious remains from profanations by the Infidels, the four sarcophagi, wich contain the remains of the Saints of Provence, had been buried in 716.

Prince Charles was overjoyed to have found the crypt, the sarcophagi, and the remains. He thus wanted to construct a magnificent monument and an adjacent convent of Dominicans to guard the remains. The excavation took place in 1279, the remains were raised in 1280, and construction on the convent and basilica began in 1295-1296.

Charles II, who became Count of Provence upon the death of his father, Charles I, envisioned an enormous temple, in order to house the vast numbers of pilgrims he imagined would come.

The Saint-Pilon, presumed meeting place of Saint Maximin and Saint Mary Magdalene (on the road from Saint-Maximin to the Sainte-Baume)

In the Crypt of the basilica, the head of the most venerable of saints, Mary Magdalene.

For this considerable project, an architect was contacted, but not retained (Mathieu). By special charter, the King Charles II, entrusted the design and plan of Saint Maximin to "Magister Petrus Gallicus, protomagister operum curiae". But at this time he was known simply as Pierre d'Agincourt. Did he ever come to Saint Maximin? This is another question…

The construction carried on until 1301, halted for a few years, and started again in 1305 under the supervision of the architect Jean Baudici. The apse was finished in 1320 with the completion of the first girder of the three naves.

Great generosity was shown on the part of the successors of Charles II, King Robert, Queen Jeanne, King René, and also on the part of "Les Souverains Pontifes", to complete this magnificent shrine. But il is mainly thanks to the endless efforts of the Dominicans that this immense work was accomplished.

The following four girders were raised during the 14th century between 1330 and 1345. The building at this time stopped at the sixth girder. But in 1404, Jean le Maingre, nicknamed "Boucicault", Marechal of France, wished to have the sixth girder of the northern nave above the crypt edified, along with the adjacent buttresses. Jacques Caille, a mason from Nans, was chosen to direct this project. But the main and southern naves still stopped at the sixth girder. Finally, in 1508, under Louis XII, with the help of Father Damiani, Prior of the convent at the time, the construction of the sixth girder, which had begun one hundred years earlier under "Boucicault", was recommenced and finished in 1513 by the architect Hugues Caillat, from Marseille.

Basilica, West façade and main entrance (unfinished)

Basilica, main entrance

The Prior and the Dominicans decided to finish the church and contracted an architect named Pierre Garcin and his father Jean Garcin, from Jouques, for the three final girders and the doors of the lateral naves. All was finished, as it stands today, in 1532 after several interruptions by the Plague.

However, the bell tower and the main entrance were never finished.

"The Basilica of Saint Maximin, with the whole of its monastic buildings, with its lateral buttresses, ten on each side holding the arches which prop up the vaulted ceilings... with its strange, mythic gargoyles, remnants of the past... with its small turrets which serve as stairways flanking the apse, one of which serves as a bell tower... the basilica offers a plain view of majesty... Its west façade, with its rough, uneven stones which look as though they await the hand of the mason to return to finish them, resembles a ruin.

But when we cross the threshold of this building, we find ourselves brusquely, and without warning, facing a grandiose architecture which seizes us by the majesty of its order and the strength of its execution. It is a gothic vessel of marvellous beauty and incomparable purity of line, of an elegance and lightness of form… By the prodigious soaring pillars, it imposes nobility from its vaulted ceilings and above all, from the supreme harmony of proportion, despite its sculptural bareness, pushed to the farthest limits, it remains inimitably beautiful"[2]

Baptismal fount

One of the four bells of the basilica

Soaring pillars

DESCRIPTION

The basilica consists of three naves and their adjoining chapels. Here are the dimensions:

Length of the large nave ....72.60 m
Length of the side naves ....64.20 m
Height of the large
nave under the vault .... approx. 29 m
Height of the side naves ....16.60 m
Height of the chapels ....10.25 m
Width of the 3 naves and chapels .....37.20 m
Width of the large nave between
the columns ....13.20 m
Width of the side naves ....6.90 m
Depth of the chapels ....5.10 m

The large nave contains nine girders, the side naves, eight, each of which corresponds to a chapel. The "Fenestrado Baselico" sung by Mistral did not count less than 66 openings, of which, 44 let light in, today. The windows of the chapels are walled-in behind the altars and altarpieces. The bays are currently made of uncoloured glass. The beautiful stained-glass windows, works of Didier de la Porte, native of Langres and habitant of Sollies (Var), were put in, in 1521, and broken during the Religious wars (end of the 16th Cent.).

Cornerstone
(south side)

Altar of the rosary (south side)

THE APSE

Nothing in this church compares to the seven-sides apse, five sides of which are pierced with a double row of superimposed openings at a great height, separated only by a transom, and that, today, finds itself invaded by marble from the time of Louis XIV.

Inside the apse, the altar spreads itself out with magnificence and majesty. The main altar is made of mottled marble enhanced by gold medallions and, like that of the "Glory", "The Angels", and "The Holy Trinity", is the work of Joseph Lieutaud. Lieutaud came from La Ciotat, he was a student of Bernin in Roma and a disciple of Pierre Puget (1678-1682).

The altar is topped by a beautiful urn made of porphyry, created in Rome by Sylvius Calce. Its lid is topped by a statue of the Algarde in golden bronze. It was brought to Saint Maximin and given to the basilica by the Archbishop of Avignon, Dominique de Marinis, dominican. It was blessed by Pope Urbain VIII in 1634. Some of the relics of Saint Mary Magdalene were transported there, February 5, 1660, in the presence of Louis XIV and the royal court. Beautiful stuccos carpet the walls of the apse: They are the work of J.A. Lombard, master mason of Carpentras, established in Marseille (1684).

Two bas-reliefs decorate the left and right walls of the sanctuary. To the north, the first one in white marble, was brought from Rome, by an unknown sculptor, and represents the rapture of Mary of Magdala.

To the south, the second in fired clay, by Lieutaud,

La Gloire. Modern stained-glass window

shows her last communion. One magnificent communion table in marble seals off the principal choir area. Three pictures relative to the story of Mary of Magdala are part of the decoration of the apse: In the middle is illustrated the penitent in the Sainte Baume; to the right, she is throwing away her jewels; to the left, she is bending over the empty sepulchre of the resuscitated Jesus. These pictures are the works of Boisson (Buisson), painter from Aix.

Mary Magdalene
painted by André Boisson.

Next page: Mary Magdalene
at the sepulchre,
painted by André Boisson

Door to the choir area

Medallion on the left door:
The ecstasy of Saint Dominique

Appearance of Saints Peter and Paul to Saint Dominique.
Below: Saint Peter of Verona, Martyr

WOODWORKS OF THE CHOIR AREA

In the choir area, we will not stop admiring the woodworking in sculpted walnut, including 94 stalls which move from left to right in two rows, against a sort of chancel where 22 medallions are sculpted, ten on each side immediately above the stalls and two above the chancel. These medallions represent the saints of the Dominican order (1681-1692). The sculptures are the work of various artists, most notably among them, the lay brother, Vincent Funel, of the convent of Saint Maximin, and Jean-Baptiste Oléri, from Marseille. He is also personnaly responsible for the crucifix and the two beautiful angels placed above the door of the choir loft, and likewise, all the statuettes that decorate (or decorated, several of them having been stolen) the various passages mounting to the stalls. He is also the sculptor of the two lateral doors of the choir area and of the statues which ornate the altars of the chapels supporting the back side of the choir area. The medallions were made by the chisel of brother Vincent Funel.

THE PULPIT

In the large nave, we admire the monumental pulpit, in sculpted walnut, retracing, in seven medallions curving up the ramp, the story of the conversion of Mary magdalene. She is wearing the costume of the time of Louis XV. Above the abat-voie (voice shade or sounding board), Mary Magdalene is carried by the angels; below, the dove of the Holy Spirit, in golden wood. Sculptured in haut-reliefs under the pulpit are tributes to the four evangelists. The pulpit is due to another talented Dominican, brother Louis Gudet, who finished it in 1756.

THE ORGAN

Above the main entrance, the historic Grandes Orgues, known the world over. This organ was built by brother Jean-Esprit Isnard, Dominican from the convent of Tarascon, one of the most talented organ makers of his time. We read the following inscription, by his own hand: "This organ was made by brother J. Isnard and his nephew, in the year 1773".
It is composed of a double case, 4 keyboards, 43 stops, and 2960 pipes.
Behind the organ, on the wall, we can see the drawing of what would have been the large ogival opening of the rose window, showing through the west façade, had it been finished.

THE CHAPELS
Southern Nave
To the right on entering:

First chapel: Dedicated to the Assumption of the Blessed Virgin.

Second chapel: A mediocre copy of a Rubens, the adoration of the shepherds. On the walls: Four large subjects painted on wood, 15th century.

Third chapel: Statue of the Vierge Blanche, in marble from carrare. It was offered by the city of Genes to the Capuchins convent. When the revolution in 1789 closed and then destroyed their convent, the statue of the Virgin was brought to the basilica.

Fourth chapel: Saint Dominique. This chapel, steeply gradated like that of Saint Magdalene to which it corresponds in the north nave, is decorated on the inside and outside by frescos from the 17th century. Beautiful painting representing Saint Dominique in ecstasy.

Fifth chapel: saint François d'Assise. The altar and altarpiece belonged to the Capucins convent. They were brought to the Basilica after the Revolution. A modern version of "the Nativity" is kept in this chapel.

The pulpit

Sixth chapel: The Sacred Heart (exhibition of photographs of the famous shape of Saint-Louis d'Anjou).

Seventh chapel: Saint Joseph

Eighth chapel: Saint Michael

Across, against the woodworks of the choir area: Chapel of Saint Anne.

At the far end of each of the side chapels is an altar and altarpiece, remarkable for various reasons. The Rosary one, in the southern nave, with the statue of Notre Dame du Rosaire, is the work of Balthasar Maunier, sculptor from the 17th century (1667-1671). The front of this altar is occupied by a bas-relief in golden wood from the 16th century A.D. It made part of the old main altar begun in 1536 by Jean Beguin, painter from Saint Maximin, and, painted by his brother-in-law Sebastien Lecouvreur. In four distinct subjects, it retraces the life of the penitent Mary Magdalene.

White Virgin in the chapel
of Notre-Dame de l'Esperance

Ceiling of the sacristy

Notre-Dame de Lourdes
Across above: Virgin with child
Across below: Gilt virgin

Saint Catherine of Sienna
and Saint Rose of Lima

Above:
Saint Antoine of Padoue

Below:
Saint Mary Magdalene

Next pages:
The altarpiece of the Passion
by Antoine Ronzen.

Northern Nave
To the left on entering

First chapel: Saint Peter (Reception)

Second chapel: Saint Blaise (baptismal founts) and statue of John the Baptist.

Third chapel: Saint Louis of Anjou, or of Brignoles, son of Charles II d'Anjou.

Fourth chapel: Saint Magdalene and relics of saints. Frescoed murals from the 17th century. Painting: Mediocre copy of "Magdalene" by Lebrun. Ancient doors of reliquaries.

Fifth chapel: Passage to the convent. Exhibition of photographs of the Dominicans at the convent, and in the basilica.

Sixth chapel: Saint Eloi.

Seventh chapel: Saint John the Baptist. Crucifixion from the 17th century and a painting of the descent from the cross (Spanish school, 16th Cent.).

Eighth chapel: Saint Maximin. Entrance to the sacristy.
Opposite, against the woodworks of the choir area: Altar of the Spirits of Purgatory. Saint Thomas Aquinas.

THE ALTARPIECE OF THE CRUCIFIX

The absidal chapel of the northern nave is occupied by a work, from the 16th century, recalling all the scenes from the Passion of Christ, in 18 medallions grouped around the large central painting: The crucifixion. This is the chief work attributed to Antoine Ronzen, of the Venitian school. He was helped considerably in this work by a painter from the Brea dynasty, another Antoine. The essential collaboration appears in the "Mise au Tombeau" which is placed in front of the altar (1517-1520).

The Dominican, represented in this "Mise au Tombeau", who we believed for a long time to be Father Damiani, priest of the convent, is actually the donator of this altarpiece, Jacques de Baume, Seigneur of Semblançay. The latter is dressed in the Dominican costume and carries, attached to his belt, a purse, signifying his role as superintendent of finances.

Having been made to hang by King François 1st, the religious of the convent added a monk's rosary to the purse of the hung man. The overcharge was discovered and abolished at the time of the restoration of the paintings by the service of the Beaux-Arts after the last war..

Robe of Saint Louis of Anjou

The Robe: the purification of the Virgin. Presentation to Simeon

THE CAPE OF SAINT LOUIS OF ANJOU

It is displayed in the sacristy, an object of inestimable artistic value. This cape from 1296 was bequeathed, we think, by the saint minor brother, Bishop of Toulouse, to the Dominican convent founded by his father. The back side is made of woven gold cloth and the subjects embroidered with silk of many colours.

It is divided into 30 compartments, representing the life of the Holy Virgin Mary and the Passion of Christ. Unfortunately, in the 18th century A.D., it was cut, shortened, and deprived.

Are also kept in the second southern chapel, four large paintings on wood from the 15th century, representing life-sized figures: Saint Laurent, martyr; Saint Antoine; hermit; Saint Sebastien and Saint Thomas Aquinas.

The first and the last are attributed to blessed André Abellon, Dominican born in Saint Maximin, who died in Aix in the odour of sanctity (1450).

Details of the Robe of Saint Louis of Anjou

The other two were poorly repainted and disfigured. These four subjects were part of the little altarpiece situated in the chapel of Saint Jean, in the northern nave, where can still be seen the "prédelle" of the altar of this same altarpiece.

It is certain that at the place of the current entrance to the choir area, was a rood loft which rested to the right and left on the two corresponding pillars. We attribute its construction to the generosity of the Archbishop of Aix, Pierre Filioli (1520).

Father Reboul, in his work "Chronique", mentions the donor: "Monseigneur Pierre Filioli had a very beautiful jubé made at the front of the choir for singing l'Epitre and l'Evangile in great solemnity", and for exposing the remains of Saint Mary Magdalene on holy days, as was also witnessed by a pilgrim of distinction in 1578: Father Serafino Razzi, a member of the "Frères Prêcheurs of Italy".

Four large paintings on wood, once part of the altarpiece (destroyed) from the chapel of Saint John

" Noli me tangere "

" Ne me touche point,
car je ne suis pas retourné vers mon père,
mais allez à mes frères
et dites-leur : je monte vers mon père et votre
père, vers mon dieu et votre dieu. "
Jean, chap. XX, 16.18

THE CRYPT

The crypt is the heart of the basilica. There have rested, during many centuries, the remains of our precious saints of Provence, our first missionaries. The current vault is not the original one; it was redone at the time of the construction of the great church and stands at the same level.

It holds four very beautiful sarcophagi, three of which are from the 4th century and the other from the 5th. For a long time one thought Saint Mary Magdalene's sarcophagus to be made of alabaster. It is made of finely grained marble, even rarer, marble which comes from the imperial quarries of the sea of Marmara, close to Constantinople.

One was brought to Saint Maximin. For who was this made, if not for Saint Mary Magdalene? It is this tomb of Mary of Magdala which is used as an altar in front of the holy saint. The other sarcophagi are those of Saint Maximin, Saint Sidoine, and Saints Marcelle and Suzanne.

Details of the sarcophagus

At the back of the crypt, around the head of Mary Magdalene, are four polished slabs built into the wall, engraved with simple, single-lined figures. We believe these slabs to be from the 6th century. They represent:

The Virgin Mary at the Temple,
Daniel in the Lion's Den,
The Sacrifice of Abraham,
The Chaste Suzanne.

A crystal tube, sealed at both ends by a vermeil snap, finds itself attached to the large shrine of Mary Magdalene. This we have always considered as being the "Noli me tangere" (don't touch me), a shred of flesh or bone tissue from the frontal bone of Mary of Magdala, where the Saviour placed his fingers the morning of the Resurrection. This piece of flesh was detached at the time of one of the formal acknowledgements of the remains, in February 1789.

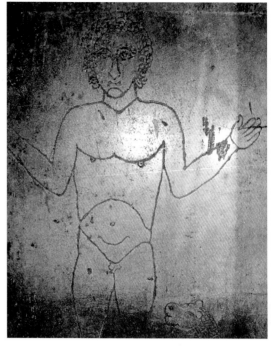

Daniel in the lions den

" Noli me Tangere ":
relic of Saint Mary Magdalene

Detail of the sarcophagus

THE SACRISTY

This annex of the church is in the eastern wing of the convent.

It is of the same age as the apse. Its ogival vaults are remarkably noble, but it is unfortunate that the religious of old, altered its primitive character by enlarging the windows, decorating the vaults with frescos (1548), and breaking the same ribbed vaults in order to dress the walls in wood-work cabinets, though very beautiful in their own right, which we owe to the talent of Brother Louis Gudet, creator of the bishop's throne (1752).

The cape of Saint Louis is kept in the chapiere beneath the central picture.

Page to the left:
the head of Mary Magdalene,
remains of the saint.

This page below: pieta from
15th Cent. (kept in the sacristy).

This page above:
Virgin in wood in the sacristy.

In Mary magdalen's chapel opposite the crypt, the two reliquaries cabinets have just been restored. They probably are from seventeenth century.Yhe last inventory before the Revolution, in 1780, give the detail.

During the ransack of the basilica in 1793, the sexton Bastide mentions a total weight of 22 « quintaux de Provence » (about 800 kilograms) for reliquaries and shrines. We understand the authorities preocupation to maintain the remparts « in order to protect the relics ».

THE ROYAL DOMINICAN CONVENT

Like the Basilica, the royal convent is a work of the love and gratitude of Charles II of Anjou to the "Beneficent Magdalene" and the Order of Saint Dominique. Having decided on the construction of these two monuments, Charles obtained from Pope Boniface VIII the right to evict the monks of Saint Victor and installed, in their place, les Frères Précheurs, in recognition of their help in liberating him from the prisons in Barcelona. Effectively, Boniface VIII, recognized the truth of the discovery of the remains of Mary Magdalene, and in a bull to King Charles II the 8th of the Ides of April 1295, authorized the switch.

In this bull, the pope placed this convent under the special protection of The Saint Siege and exempted the church, with all of its dependants, from the jurisdiction of the Abbey of Saint Victor, giving to the prior the power to reform the monks upon the demand of the king.

The next day, the 7th of the Ides of April, he renewed these exemptions of jurisdiction and, according to the wishes of Charles II, instated Father Guillaume of Tonneins as prior, fixed by the king for this institution, and ordaining that future elections of the prior himself would henceforth be subject to royal approbation.

Until the revolution, the monks of the convent acted in the following way when naming a prior: They presented three names to the sovereign who would choose one, and a new prior would be elected.

The pope conferred to that prior the responsibility of the souls of all the habitants and of the territory, without having to submit to any diocese jurisdiction and without justification.

Finally, he stipulated to receive the king in procession whenever it pleased him to visit the convent, accorded to himself the title of "souverain patron".

It was always to these two bulls that the religious turned to when in question of their rights, in the following centuries. Moreover, by the third bull, again written on the 7th of the Ides of April, the pope committed the Bishop of Marseille to carry out the mandates of the first two bulls, he asked him to give to Charles II the position of the prior of Saint Maximin, through the Bishop of Sisteron, Pierre Lamanon, to whom he delegated this effect in a fourth bull, dated the 6th of the Ides of April.

Seal of Saint-Maximin-de-Provence,
18th Cent.

The Bishop of Sisteron was put in possession of the church and the priory with all the buildings and appendages, likewise that of the treasures, remains, and sacred ornaments, under threat of excommunication for any opponent. The solemn act of this installation was blessed and read in the primitive church at Saint Maximin in front of the altar of Saint Michael, in the presence of witnesses, thus we have come to know these names, it occurred the 20th of June, 1295.

Charles II had stipulated to Hugues de Vins, Seneschal of Provence, to assist the authority of the Bishops of Marseille and Sisteron in their seizure of possessions and had recommended to the bailiff and the inhabitants of Saint Maximin to lend man-power to the seneschal if it was requested. But the Benedictines abandoned without difficulty their monastery: There was no need to call for physical force to instigate the change.

Charles II had allocated considerable sums, for the upkeep of the monks and building the convent and basilica. These often fell short, causing construction to sometimes have to be stopped.

The convent, viewed from the Clos

Across: the cloister

Gallery of the cloister

CONSTRUCTION OF THE MONUMENTS

At the beginning of the work, the first and second campaigns of construction on the convent and the basilica are rigorously parallel: They begin together and they end together.

The First Campaign: 1295-1301 (approximately)
Architect of the work, author of the plans: "Protomagister Petrus Gallicus d'Agincourt".
East Wing (which stands next to the apse of the basilica and was constructed at the same time).
On the ground floor:
— the sacristy
— the chapter house
— the house of monks
— passage, stairway
On the first floor: A stairway which descended from the dormitory to the basilica, demolished today.
The roof: Covered with round tiles like those on the surrounding houses'lofts.

The Second Campaign: after 1301
Architect: Jean Baudici.
North Wing
On the ground floor:
— ex-refectory
— ex-atrium (sacristy)
— two of three bays of the ex-chapel
We can clearly see in the cloister the thrust of the high wall which corresponds to the same thrust on the basilica.
On the first floor: dormitory.

The Third Campaign: retake of the work done in the 14th century
The north wing of the convent is finished.
On the ground floor: ex-chapel.
The beautiful spiral staircase on the first floor: dormitory.
But the entrance door of the chapel, which still exists, is the work of Ricard, who, having bought the north wing at a state goods' sale by the Convention, turned this part of the building into a wine cellar

The Fourth Campaign:

All of the buildings were heightened by one floor during the reign of King René (between 1434 and 1480) in order to house 48 monks instead of 24. The cloister is without a doubt from this period. Dating also from this period is the most famous foundation of king René: The establishment of a theological, philosophical, and canonical college for the young monks of the convent, as always, "of the aim to augment the glory and honour of Saint Mary Magdalene", who he called "secretariam et solam apostolam J. Christi" (1476).

Salle capitulaire (today: restaurant salon)

Lucky well of André Abellon,
dug between 1370 and 1450,
financed by his mother Esméniarde Rosols

The chapel

This college was the object of fierce disputes between the city and the Dominicans. Therefore was founded a grammar school (1570).

The college was raised next to the north wing of the convent, adjoining the ex-house of Grimaud and spreading out to the current monument of the deads. After the revolution, it was converted first into a saltpetre factory. One part of the roof having fallen down, it was demolished in 1832.

The Fifth Campaign:

In the 17th century, caves were dug beneath the east wing. Therefore the chapter house and the sacristy were heightened.

The Sixth Campaign:

The west wing, called "the Lacordaire wing", has been constructed in several stages. During the revolution, it was bought and destroyed by Ricard, who wanted to clean up the garden of the cloister and open there a beautiful square for the use of the people of the country.

This wing and the work of the corresponding cloister-bays were reconstructed starting in 1860, under Father Lacordaire, the illustrious restorator of the order of preachers who brought back the Dominicans from Chalais (in Switzerland) to Saint Maximin in 1859. The wing was reconstructed according to the taste of the time, in "troubadour gothic".

Seventh Campaign:

"L'Hospice", the current Hotel de Ville, was raised by Franque, famous architect, in place of a first "Hostellerie des moines" (Hotel of the Monks), which, even though it sheltered so many crowned heads, was falling in ruins.

Construction from the 18th century, between 1750 and 1785.

This construction of a severe and regular style, decorated by pillars and crowned by a large pediment upon which can be seen the vestiges of the shield of France, effaced during the revolution, bears the date 1777.

The library at the time of the Dominicans

Hotel de Ville, former hostellerie of the royal convent, XVIII Century.

Lit by 26 large windows, this monument is placed to the left of the basilica. The entrance is through a tall door, which was also the main entrance to the convent, it opens onto a beautiful vestibule, semi-circular in shape, decorated with pillars and half-dome vaults, like all of the ground and first floors. To the left can be found two larger rooms of about equal dimensions. The first of these, formerly called "Salon du Roi" (King's Salon), was decorated with portraits of kings. The second served as a carpentry workshop. A bit further along, a little room was used as the office of the father priest. To the right, on entering, vis-à-vis to the "Salon du Roi", past that which was the apartment of the brother doorman and large warehouses, one follows a beautiful corridor which reaches from the west to the east, up to the large door of the cloister. It has been walled-up, but is still easily visible. This corridor has been turned into the secretariat. Across from the entrance, a majestic staircase, decorated with a remarkable rod-iron side-rail, gives access to the first floor, meant to lodge visitors of distinction. Fortunately, it is the Communauté de la Ville which made itself buyer of the large premises in 1796, and moved in. The town-council up to that point, since what time we do not know, had occupied the first floor of the house of M. Gasquet de Valette, rue de la Masse. So, the city made 200 sterling in rent every year.

Room of honour on the first floor

Large staircase

Gallery of the cloister

Even though the total construction of the convent extended through many centuries, the Dominicans were able to move in their new residence as soon as 1316. They numbered 20.

Previously, revealed the chronicle of the priors, they lived at the House of monks of Saint Victor, who had left in 1295. During the third campaign, the convent was sacked by Arnaud de Cervoles and his band of looters (1357). With the return of peace, the habitants wanted to repair their damaged ramparts. They demolished one part of the convent in order to use the material to rebuild the surrounding walls. The damage undertaken by the convent was estimated at 8.000 florins.

During the religious wars

In July of 1590, the "Ligueurs" laid siege before Saint Maximin. The prior of the convent at the time, Father Niellis, obtained from the opposing General, Martinengo, that he would not turn his forces against the convent nor the church of the saint Magdalene, saving the monument as well as the remains from almost certain destruction. The city resisted the attack with ferocious energy from behind its ramparts, and after fifteen days of siege, and having suffered 800 canon shots, pushed back the assailants. We can still see the points of impact from the bullets on the walls of the basilica. The surrounding walls are pierced with large openings.

During the century of Louis XIV, in order to repair the damage the convent had suffered at the hands of time and of men, the Dominicans, under the conduct of Father Michel Jourdain, their fifty-second prior (1653-1656), transformed the house in one notable and perhaps unfortunate way. The roof needed to be entirely redone: it was replaced by timbers in Mansard's fashion, unknown in Provence until that time.

Remarkable work, but with some serious and unavoidable inconveniences. Actually, under violent gusts of wind, the steeply inclined tiles move, and eventually detach completely.

Restored as well, at the time of Father Jourdain, is the lovely spiral staircase. The large bedrooms were converted into individual cells, built in two rows separated by a large corridor.

The French Revolution expulsed the faithful from their convent. They got over the threshold in March of 1791. Some went soon after to other countries, others renounced the communal life, but stayed on the national territory.

"The vast buildings rest sometimes empty and deserted. Under the Terror (1793), the cells and floors were transformed into a prison for suspects of the contrée". On the first floor, the little refectory became the local revolutionary club.

Timbers of the royal convent (details of carpentry)

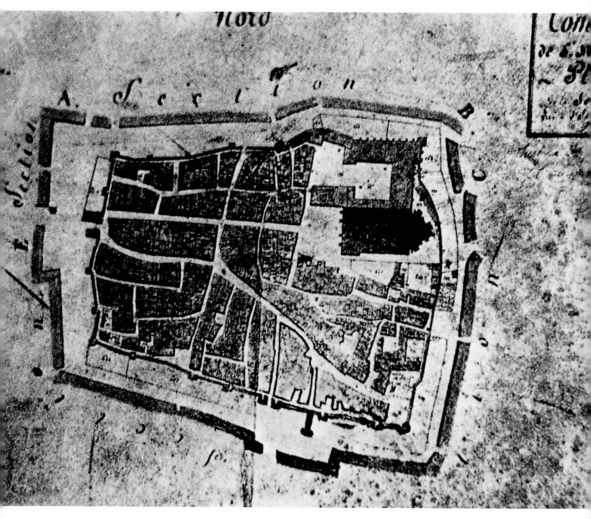

Plan of Saint Maximin (beginning of the 19th Cent.)

"It is there that a young man, destined to play a historic role in the Consulat, Lucien Bonaparte, made his first speeches. The large refectory was converted for him into a music hall".

"Finally, July 6 1796, we proceed to the sale of the monastic buildings. One part converted into individual habitation, and the rest more or less left abandoned. The cloister will be victim of degrading profanations. In the solitary corridors, the birds of night will be heard to sing their gloomy songs, and in the devastated courtyard, the games of children from the neighbourhood will be the only bit of animation".

It is to this moral and physical ruin that Father Lacordaire will have to give back life enthusiasm and ferveur in buying the old convent of Saint Maximin on April 5, 1859.

After the departure of the Dominicans for Toulouse in November of 1957, the royal convent became the College of "Contemporary Exchange", and then "L'Hotellerie du Couvent Royal".

NOTES

1. (Mc XVI-15) (Mt XXVIII-19).
2. Louis Rostan, "Notice de l'église", pp. 76 à 79.
3. Conclusion de l'analyse du marbre par le Pr Astre, de la Faculté des sciences de Toulouse, en 1953. Le Pr Astre fut le spécialiste de l'analyse des marbres européens.
4. Louis Rostan, "Monographie du couvent", pp. 23 à 35.
5. Fernand Cortez, "La révolte des paysans", p. 5.
6. Louis Rostan, "Monographie du couvent", pp. 77 à 79.

Texte : Solange ROSTAN et Michel MONCAULT.

Illustrations photographiques :

Véronique GUÉRIN-POITRASSON

sauf
Michel GRANIOU (P. 32 et 33)
HENRI DARIES (Couverture. P. 42. 43. et P. 51)

Achevé d'imprimer en Mai 2003
Dépôt légal à parution

Imprimé en C.E.E.